The Simon de Montf

SIMON DE MO

PATRICK ROOKE

First published in Great Britain in 2008 by lulu.com
www.lulu.com

ISBN: 978-0-9558486-0-5

www.simondemontfort.org

This plaque adorns the wall of the House of Representatives in Washington D.C.

CONTENTS

The marriage of Simon de Montfort to Eleanor, Henry III's sister

Chapter One   AN IMMIGRANT TO REMEMBER

Who was Simon de Montfort? The name is probably as familiar to anyone with a passing interest in British history as that of Alfred the Great, Francis Drake or Christopher Wren, but there it ends. The majority of such persons know little or nothing about his significance in this country's story, where or why a university has in recent years been named after him or what prompted the Speaker of the House of Commons to go to Evesham in 1965 to commemorate his death some seven hundred years after the event.

Medieval chroniclers, such as his contemporary Matthew Paris, portray Simon as a charismatic and complex figure. A man of contradictions he was forthright and enigmatic, chivalrous, yet at times dictatorial, an able military strategist who also cultivated the friendship and guidance of some of Western Europe's foremost religious leaders. Ironically, he was a critic of England's king, Henry III, for the favouritism he showed towards foreigners while being a favoured foreigner himself.

Simon was born in France of aristocratic parents about the year 1208. Although the family home was at Montfort l'Amaury, 30 miles west of Paris, it seems likely that the young Montfort spent much of his childhood with his parents in the south of the country. Little is known of his early years, the consequence no doubt of the fact that he was the third of four sons - Amaury and Guy preceding him - and must have seemed to any chronicler of the time someone unlikely to merit attention.

His father, also named Simon, was primarily a soldier. He won praise for his prowess whilst on the Fourth Crusade (1202-4). The reputation gained here was to be tarnished, however, shortly after the birth of his son Simon, by the ruthlessness he employed when leading a French army against the stronghold of the Albigensian heretics in the Languedoc region of France.

During the twelfth century the kings of England had greatly extended their domains in France. In particular this expansion came about as a result of the marriage of Henry II to Eleanor of Aquitaine. What both Henry and his son John were unwilling to admit was that they were not independent rulers of these newly acquired provinces, but only held them as fiefs of the king of France. This tide of territorial growth was to receive a humiliating reversal early in the following century when King John's forces were defeated by those of Philip II of France with the loss of most of the earlier gains. When John's son came to the throne as Henry III all that was left for him on the French mainland was Gascony.

Although Simon could have been little more than ten when his father died, being killed at the siege of Toulouse in 1218, the influence that Simon the elder had on Simon the boy must have been considerable. This was to become evident not only in the fascination that he was to show for military ventures but akso by the way, like his father, he was to seek out the friendship of distinguished churchmen. The ambitious streak that the young Montfort was to exhibit can also be seen mirrored in the behaviour of the parent. These attributes, important though they may have been in contributing to Simon's personality, do not directly explain how a French younger son, with few prospects, was able to make such a mark on the affairs of alien England.

The chain of events that eventually led to Simon coming to England began with his grandmother, Amicia. To be more exact it was initiated in 1204 by the death of her childless brother, Robert de Beaumont, earl of Leicester. Through Amicia, as co-heiress of Robert's estate, the elder Simon was to inherit a claim to the earldom but one from which, being a French subject, he was ineligible to benefit. To resolve the immediate inheritance problem King John, in 1215, made Ranulf, earl of Chester, keeper of the disputed Leicester lands, an arrangement that was converted into a life grant in 1227 by Henry III.

Amaury, as the eldest surviving Montfort, pursued the family's right to the earldom, which he argued had now passed to him. His efforts were to no avail. In the first place, as constable of France, he too was barred from holding the English title and in the second, as the Leicester domains had been placed in Ranulf's keeping, they could not be given to another until he relinquished them.

Faced with this situation Amaury turned to his brother, Simon, who he now saw as next in line, Guy having died in 1220. In the negotiations that followed, probably in 1229, Amaury agreed to exchange any rights he might have to the honour of Leicester for Simon's inherited lands in France. In addition a large sum of money was almost certainly paid to Amaury by Simon, a transaction that would have helped to lay the foundation of the latter's subsequent financial difficulties.

Eager to press his claim Simon now came to England. He did so at a time when Henry was about to embark on a campaign to recapture Normandy, a venture which was to prove a failure. The readiness of Simon to assist the English king in this undertaking was accompanied by an assurance from Henry that the Montfort claim to the Leicester lands would be respected once they were released by Ranulf. Not prepared to wait for their keeper's death, the ambitious Simon entered into discussions with Ranulf and succeeded in persuading him to transfer them straight away, money (once again) most likely being used as an inducement.

In August 1231, as good as his word, Henry confirmed Simon's rights to the honour of Leicester. This, however, only granted him ownership of the lands, not the earldom of Leicester. For the receipt of that title he would have to wait several years.

When Simon journeyed to Rome in 1238 to ensure that Pope Gregory did not declare his recent marriage invalid he probably crossed the Channel in a ship similar to this

Chapter Two   SIMON SETTLES IN

Simon was quick to establish himself as part of the English scene. In this he was helped by the king who made him welcome. Later Henry was to value Simon's military expertise, but initially it was probably out of respect for his celebrated father that he was drawn to the newcomer. Two other factors that may have led Henry to cultivate a friendship with Simon were, firstly, their closeness in age - Henry was born in 1207 - and secondly, that Simon was a Frenchman and England's king was already earning a reputation for rewarding foreigners.

The relationship between Montfort and monarch remained close throughout the 'thirties. Thereafter it was to deteriorate into one in which concord and hostility were to alternate dramatically. When the latter was dominant Simon's financial problems were often a root cause of the friction. Even during his early years in England money difficulties began to bedevil him. His modest baronial living, as Simon viewed the income from his newly-gained lands, was reduced further in value by the need to pay off debts incurred in claiming his inheritance. Both ambitious and resourceful, Simon saw two possible ways of improving his position. The first of these was by upgrading his social status through the acquisition of the title, earl of Leicester. The second, was by succeeding in making a profitable marriage.

Simon's initial hopes of marrying a French wealthy bride were doomed to failure, at least two attempts to do so being vetoed by Blanche of Castile, the queen mother of France and, for a time, the country's regent, who was unwilling to see French domains fall into the hands of someone who was now paying allegiance to the king of England. But such disappointments were to be short-lived for, in January 1238, Simon married Henry's sister, Eleanor.

Although the wedding delighted Simon, demonstrating as it did how highly regarded he was by the king, the circumstances surrounding it were shrouded in mystery. Far from being an occasion for widespread celebration, the ceremony was conducted secretively in a small chamber in Westminster and not by the Archbishop of Canterbury, as might have been expected, but by one of the king's chaplains. Even Richard, Eleanor's brother, was unaware of what was taking place.

When news of the marriage became public it raised a storm of anger amongst many of the barons who argued, with some justification, that Henry's failure to consult them about such an important issue was in breach of the Magna Carta. Eleanor, now aged 23, had already been married to William Marshal, the powerful earl of Pembroke, who had died in 1231. Many magnates pointed out that this union had been approved only after lengthy discussions had produced their consent.

The outcome of Eleanor's marriage to Simon was further complicated by the fact that, following the death of her first husband, she had taken a vow of chastity before the Archbishop of Canterbury. Any attempt to ignore the importance of this act was certain to be misguided, though the low-key nature of the wedding ceremony, timed whilst Archbishop Edmund was in Rome, suggests that Henry had hoped to ward off Church protests by presenting the union as a *fait accompli*. The resulting furore must have exceeded Henry's worst misgivings for it was so great that within a few weeks of the marriage Simon was forced to journey to Rome in order to ensure that the Pope did not declare it invalid. At the same time Henry wrote to the Pontiff to reinforce Simon's pleading. Their anxiety about the reaction of the Pope to the marriage is indicative of the strength of papal power at this period of history.

The manner of Simon's marriage to Eleanor certainly aroused controversy, but there is little doubt that the relationship was a successful one. They were to work well together and each appears to have been faithful to the other.

Simon returned to England towards the end of 1238. The months that followed were to find him basking in the king's favour. He was pre-eminent amongst Henry's advisers. In February 1239 this prominence was given public acknowledgement when Henry, at last, conferred upon him the title of earl of Leicester. A few weeks before this took place the king had attended the baptism of the Montforts' first son at Kenilworth when, significantly, the baby had been christened Henry and not with one of the family's traditional names. Not long afterwards Simon was to be one of three earls present at the baptism of Henry's first born, Edward.

This harmony between the two brothers-in-law, however, was to be short-lived. Despite Simon's outward success he was still wrestling with financial worries, the pressure of which led him into making an ill-judged presumption on the king's goodwill.

Henry III (left) and Edward, victor of Evesham, depicted on a choir screen in York Minster

Chapter Three   TROUBLED RELATIONS

The seeds of trouble between Henry and Simon were sewn in 1238 when Peter of Dreux, count of Brittany, charged Simon with the repayment of a substantial sum of money that he had borrowed from him. Peter claimed that he needed this in order to finance going on crusade. The demand was backed by the Pope who threatened Simon with excommunication if the debt was not honoured.

Unable to find the money himself Simon arranged to transfer a significant part of the debt to Thomas of Savoy, the queen's uncle, thereby ensuring Peter of the funds he required. Unwisely, when negotiating the transaction with Thomas, Simon named Henry as security for the money without first seeking his agreement that he would act as such. Not surprisingly, when the king discovered what had happened he was furious, the more so as he had recently given Simon money to cover his expenses in Rome.

The king's rage was first evident in August 1239 when Simon and Eleanor were in London for the churching of the queen following the birth of her son, Edward. Accusing him of falsifying the use of his monarch's name, Henry barred Simon, along with Eleanor, from attending the ceremony. Even more shocking was his announcement that he had only agreed to his sister's marriage to Simon the previous year when he had learnt that she had been seduced by him. If true this might well account for the secretive nature of the wedding arrangements. In addition it would cast a different light on how Eleanor had come to break her vow of chastity, as well as explaining Henry's unpopular unilateral decision to sanction the union on the grounds that he wished to see the event over and done with as quickly as possible and with the minimum of publicity.

Despite the weight of the circumstantial evidence against Simon the truth of Henry's accusations is far from established. If the sole reason for his approval of the marriage had been out of consideration for his disgraced sister, why did Henry show Simon such favoured treatment in the period immediately following it? Would someone who could not be trusted to behave properly with his sister be the kind of person that a monarch would depend upon as a key figure in his government?

Although Henry denounced Simon for being a seducer and perjurer, it may well have been his brother-in-law's apparent disregard for the generosity that he had shown towards him that was the main cause of his hostile outburst. So great was Henry's rage that Simon, along with Eleanor (who was pregnant with their second son, another Simon) were forced to flee to France, fearful that the king would commit him to the Tower of London.

Well aware of Simon's monetary difficulties Henry took pleasure in levying £1,000 from Montfort's estate in order that Thomas of Savoy could be reimbursed. This caused a particular problem for Simon as he was now trying to gather funds to go on crusade. In order to obtain these he was forced to sell some of his lands, thus further weakening his financial base.

Henry's anger, intense though it had clearly been, cooled surprisingly quickly. Upon Simon's brief return to England in the spring of 1240 in order to finalise his plans for going to the Holy Land, and some nine months since his hasty departure across the Channel, he was reconciled with the king.

The fragile nature of this reunion was shown in 1242 when, his crusading over, Simon was summoned to join Henry in his attempt to recover the French province of Poitou. The disastrous end to this campaign prompted Simon to remark that as a result of its mismanagement Henry deserved to be locked up in prison, a comment not appreciated by the king.

That their quarrel was not re-opened was largely due to the conciliatory behaviour of Henry. When the earl returned from France in 1243 Henry did his utmost to help Simon and Eleanor with their finances. He pardoned a total of around £2,000 of the earl's debts; in February 1244 he gave Simon custody of Kenilworth Castle to become his main residence; and most significantly, perhaps, for it was to be the source of contention through the years ahead, he arranged for the payment to Eleanor of a dower as William Marshal's widow.

Why, we must ask, did Henry show such mood swings when dealing with Simon? His reconciliation with the earl and subsequent acts of generosity may well have been prompted by his realization that, awkward customer though Simon might be, he was now a member of the royal family. At the same time, and probably the more important, was an appreciation by the king that he needed both the advice and active support of his brother-in-law.

Although less energetic than his father, King John, Henry was keen to regain the Plantagenet lands that his parent had lost in France. To do this he needed both adequate funds and the support of his barons, neither of which were in plentiful supply when it came to embarking on major undertakings. To compensate for these deficiencies it must have seemed to Henry, anxious to enhance England's influence abroad, that he needed a person, close to the Crown, with military acumen, the ability to raise a significant number of troops when required and with powerful contacts in Europe. Such a person was Simon de Montfort.

The earl, of course, had needs too, to be set against those of the king. For him, as already noted, ambition was a dominant drive. Initially this was motivated by the urge to succeed in an alien land but, with marriage, providing for his growing family became a more pressing requirement. By 1244 he already had four sons - a further son and daughter were to follow. Simon was to become increasingly alarmed by the realization that most of his family's income was derived from Eleanor's lands, monies that would cease to be available when she died, either to him or to their children. In consequence a great deal of his life seems to have been obsessed with trying to bolster his financial resources, as much to safeguard the future of his children as to benefit himself. This determination to prosper was to lead, more and more, to disputes with Henry. Despite the forces that attracted the brothers-in-law to each other there were others that repelled. Ultimately the latter were to prove the more powerful.

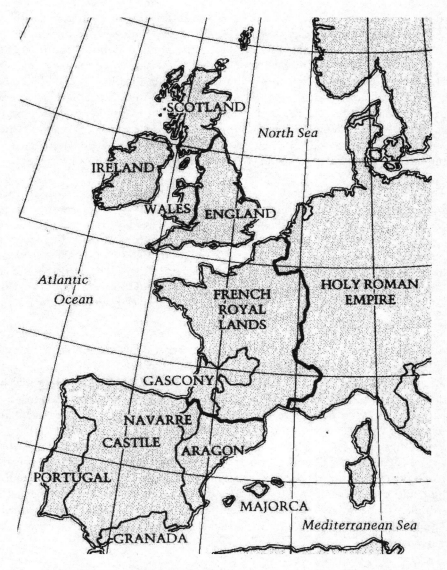

Map of Europe showing English and French lands in the thirteenth century

Chapter Four   GASCONY

By 1248 Simon was acknowledged as a formidable soldier, though exactly on what this reputation was based is not clear. Although he did engage in some fierce fighting at Saintes during the ill-fated Poitou venture (1242), the amount of action he saw while on crusade (1241) or when campaigning with Henry in Normandy (1230) and Wales (1245) was probably minimal. The king certainly valued his services for when Gascony, England's last remaining province in France, came under threat it was to Simon that he turned appointing him in May 1248 his lieutenant there for a period of 7 years. As such Simon was to have control of all monies necessary to maintain the defence of the province, while Henry would cover the cost of the upkeep of its castles.

The task confronting Simon was not an easy one. Within Gascony itself there was a populace that was restless, disorderly and ill-disposed towards paying allegiance to a foreign king. Even more menacing, from outside its borders, was a threat from hopeful claimants to Gascony's throne, notably the kings of Navarre, Castile and Aragon. A third element that the new lieutenant would have to deal with was the expiry of a five year truce that Henry had agreed with the king of France in 1243, a circumstance that no doubt both stimulated the internal unrest and encouraged the aspirations of the neighbouring monarchs.

Simon's first concern upon arriving in Gascony was to negotiate an extension of the truce with King Louis IX. Once this was successfully accomplished he was able to turn to the King of Navarre, the most vocal of the claimants. The discussions that followed also bore fruit, the King of Navarre agreeing that his dispute with Henry should go to arbitration. With these problems solved, at least for the time being, the way was now clear for Simon to deal with the remaining task of restoring order to the province.

From the outset it was apparent that Simon was going to rule with an iron fist. Acting with the authority of a contract that said nothing about the powers that he could or could not use, Simon meted out harsh justice to all he viewed as troublemakers. Many Gascons were imprisoned without trial; powerful opponents faced the loss of their castles and were often held captive until ransomed.

The furore that his policies aroused in Gascony soon led to complaints reaching Henry's ears, much to his annoyance. Amongst the protesters was Gaston de Béarn, a cousin of England's queen. When, late in 1249, Simon seized de Béarn and put him in prison, Henry promptly overruled his lieutenant and ordered the captive's release.

This new cause of friction between monarch and earl was to be accompanied by another, not so novel - difficulties over finance. It had soon become evident that neither Henry nor Simon had sufficient funds to meet the demands of his role as identified in their initial agreement. The money that Simon was able to extract from the Gascons was inadequate to cover defence costs and the expenditure the king needed to maintain the province's castles was beyond his means.

Matters came to a head in December 1251 when Simon made a brief visit to England. During his absence a revolt broke out in Gascony, which Henry hurriedly claimed was the outcome of Simon's repressive government. In consequence he refused him permission to return there to put down the rising. To make Simon's position even more untenable Henry both rejected his lieutenant's claim to be reimbursed for the expenses he had incurred in the province and refused to meet the cost of maintaining its castles as originally agreed. When Simon threatened to seize these castles in order to offset his losses the tension between the two rose dramatically. Henry was particularly alarmed by these developments as, having recently bequeathed Gascony to his son Edward, he saw Simon's threat, if carried out, as one that could jeopardise his son's inheritance.

The situation between the two deteriorated still further in May 1252 when Simon found himself facing an inquiry before the king and barons in the refectory of Westminster Abbey. This trial, for this is what it amounted to, lasted a month. Simon was accused by the Archbishop of Bordeaux, and other Gascons present, of brutality, illegal imprisonment and extorting money unjustifiably. Henry, even more vindictively, called Simon a traitor, to which the earl retorted: "That word is a lie and were you not my sovereign it would be an ill hour for you when you dared utter it".

Denying all the charges he argued that he had done his best given that the king had kept him short of funds. To Henry's dismay a strong body of support emerged for Simon, amongst which was Richard of Cornwall, the king's brother. Those who backed Henry were mostly Gascons. Chroniclers reporting on what took place portrayed Simon as the injured party. As a result the king had little alternative but to declare, begrudgingly, that Simon was free of guilt.

Despite this verdict Henry was unwilling to allow Simon to resume control of the province, assuming more responsibility for that himself. Anxious to make Gascony secure for Edward he replaced Simon's severe regime with policies that were more conciliatory. To facilitate the introduction of this new approach he negotiated a settlement with his lieutenant whereby, for renouncing all claims on the province, he was to be granted a payment in excess of £5,000. However, this was not to be the end of Simon's involvement with the region.

For the earl the closing chapter in Gascony came in 1253 when rebellion once more broke out there. Led by Gaston de Béarn, in collusion with the King of Castile, the uprising endangered Henry's rule to such an extent that he urged Simon to join the force he was assembling to deal with the rebels. Reluctant to do so at first, Simon eventually joined his brother-in-law in France. Fierce fighting followed though the conflict was brought to a satisfactory conclusion less by a military victory than by the agreement that Edward would marry the half-sister of the King of Castile.

His ultimate withdrawal from Gascony brought Simon still more monetary gains the receipt of which indicates, on the one hand, his skill as a financial negotiator and, on the other, the respect that Henry still had for him both as a soldier and as an administrator.

Montfortian "Parliament" seal

Chapter Five   THE SEEDS OF REVOLT

Henry III came to the throne of England when only nine years of age. He inherited from his father, King John, a realm that had been depleted of all French holdings except that of Gascony. As he gradually assumed full kingship Henry became aware of a second legacy from his parent, constraints imposed upon the Crown by the growing power of the barons. This development had been first significantly demonstrated in 1215 by the concessions that John was forced to make to them when agreeing to the Magna Carta. The clashes between king and magnates were evident in Great Council meetings when, all too often for the extravagant Henry, his requests for the raising of additional taxation were rejected.

What particularly angered the barons, along with others of lower rank, was the way that Henry was seen to be favouring foreigners, awarding them important posts and distributing land and revenue amongst them. The monk-historian Matthew Paris complained that Henry appeared to benefit "unknown, scurrilous and undeserving foreigners, in order to inflict an irreparable wound upon the heads of his natural subjects".

One target for those who resented overseas beneficiaries was the power of the Roman Catholic Church. They maintained that thanks to his father's surrendering to Rome, Henry now ruled a kingdom that was virtually the personal property of the Pope. As a result there were large numbers of absentee clerics, mostly Italians, drawing fees for offices they did not perform, in a land they had never visited. Paris suggested that the total cost of these absentees was about £40,000 a year.

The influential relatives of Henry's French bride, Eleanor of Provence, who he married in 1236, were a further focus of unpopularity. Foremost amongst these were two of her uncles, both members of the powerful house of Savoy, who Henry had persuaded to come to England. The one, Peter, was given the honour of Richmond, while the other, Boniface, became Archbishop of Canterbury. This association with the Savoyards was to prove disastrous in 1254 when, encouraged by them, Henry accepted Pope Innocent IV's offer of the Sicilian throne for his second son, Edmund. Before this could be realized, however, Sicily would have to be seized from its Hohenstaufen rulers, requiring a campaign well beyond Henry's current means.

A second group of the king's favourites, the Lusignans, were even more disliked than the Savoyards. These were Henry's half-brothers, children of his mother's second marriage to a Poitevin prince. One of these was made earl of Pembroke, a second, the bishop-elect of Winchester. Henry tried to promote acceptance at court of both Savoyards and Lusignans by engineering marriages between them and members of leading baronial families.

Where did Simon fit into this scheme of things? After all, he was a foreigner too. Surprisingly, although his alien origins were no doubt resented by some, criticisms of them seem rarely to have been voiced. On the contrary his background worked in his favour, bringing him influential friends across Western Europe. As well as being respected as a soldier and as an administrator, this enabled him to develop yet another role, that of diplomat.

Henry capitalized on Simon's diplomatic attributes during the years from 1254 to 1257. First he despatched him to Scotland to resolve difficulties that King Alexander III, who was married to Henry's daughter Margaret, was having with a group of his own barons. That behind him, Simon spent his remaining time moving between England and France seeking to establish, with Henry's authorization, more peaceful relationships between the two kingships. An effect of this activity was to limit his involvement in affairs at home.

Did Henry encourage Simon to become involved abroad as a means of keeping him out of his way? Probably not. The king was anxious to reach a settlement with Louis IX, optimistically hoping that it might lead to a restoration of some of England's former lands in France, and clearly decided that Simon was the best negotiator available. Despite the mounting tension between Crown and barons, Henry had no cause as yet to view his brother-in-law as an ally of the latter or as someone presenting a direct challenge to his authority.

Why was Simon willing to spend so much time and energy in the role of diplomat? Partly, one suspects, because he enjoyed the influence that participation in the ensuing discussions gave him. Of greater importance to him, however, was almost certainly the possibility that negotiations with Louis might be made to work to his own financial advantage. After all, he felt no reason for being particularly grateful to Henry for the way he had treated him regarding his lieutenancy of Gascony. The arrears of payments relating to his wife's dower also rankled, especially at a time when three Lusignans had just been awarded large sums of money. Similarly he may have found it infuriating that while protesting that he could not afford to give him greater financial help, Henry was busy seeking to raise money for the unrealistic object of securing Sicily for Edmund.

Window of St Lawrence's Church in Evesham, showing Simon de Montfort and his knights hearing mass on the morning of the Battle of Evesham

Chapter Six   DEMANDS FOR REFORM

While Simon busied himself across the Channel helping to prepare the way for the Treaty of Paris, the outcome of the discussions between England and France, the dissatisfaction of the barons with the policies of Henry continued to grow until, in 1258, it erupted into a fierce confrontation between the two sides. A number of developments hastened this. One was the collapse of the king's attempt to capture the crown of Sicily for his son Edmund, a venture that he had embarked upon without consulting his Council and that was to leave him with considerable debts. Second was the mounting anger at the arrogant and lawless behaviour of the Lusignans, whom some feared were gaining too great an influence over the heir apparent, the 19 year old Edward. A third cause of discontent affected the counties where knights and lesser gentry were feeling increasingly oppressed by the ruthless money-raising methods of the Crown's appointed sheriffs.

Broken promises to improve matters, extravagant undertakings and a failure to consult his leading magnates were key factors that eventually prompted seven barons to have a showdown with the king. This took place at a Council held at Westminster in April 1258. Following a series of hot-tempered meetings Henry agreed to consider reforms. A committee of 24 members was to be set up to prepare a list of grievances for consideration at the next Council to be held at Oxford in two months time. Temporarily back in England, Simon was to become one of the leading barons who forced Henry's acceptance of these proposals.

This reform movement was to produce the biggest attack on royal powers to date. Why Simon was to identify himself so forcibly with it at this point in time can be attributed to a number of reasons. Firstly, in addition to his other attributes, Simon was a religious scholar. He counted amongst his friends and mentors such learned figures as Robert Grosseteste, Bishop of London, Adam Marsh, a leading Oxford Franciscan and Walter de Cantelupe, Bishop of Worcester. He had also, in recent years, established a close relationship with the pious Louis IX. It seems likely that the influence of such teachers, stressing as they did the importance of justice, led him to see the moral correctness of the barons' cause.

Secondly, Simon may have chosen to ally himself with the barons by way of acknowledging their support for him when he was under attack from Henry for his administration of Gascony.

Thirdly, he possibly concluded that to join the criticism of how Henry mismanaged his own financial affairs might be made to work to his advantage.

He already knew, as a result of his diplomatic activities, that the draft of the impending Treaty of Paris required leading members of the English royal family to renounce any rights they claimed they had in France. His wife's agreement to comply with this, he must have realised, could be made conditional on the receipt, at long last, of a satisfactory dower settlement, an issue that was complicated by the large number of William Marshal's heirs who were now potential contributors to any such payment.

The decisions taken by both the embryonic parliament, which met in June 1258, and subsequent assemblies are jointly known as the 'Provisions of Oxford'. Amongst these was one that led to the setting-up of a permanent Council of 15 members that was to "have the power of advising the king in good faith concerning the government of the kingdom and concerning all matters that pertain to the king or the kingdom, and in order to amend and redress everything that (it) shall consider in need of amendment or redress. It shall have authority over the Chief Justice and over all people." This Council, only three of whose members were chosen by the king, was to meet three times a year.

The proposed changes were more radical than those laid out in the Magna Carta, limiting as never before the powers of the Crown by transferring them to a standing committee, largely elected by barons and the Church. It would now choose the country's ministers in place of the monarch. Greater authority was to be given to the counties where, in each, four elected knights were to be responsible for notifying the Crown's chief legal officer, the justiciar, of any grievances in their shire.

Henry was among those who swore an oath to observe the Provisions. The refusal of the Lusignans to do likewise was to lead to their expulsion from the country, thereby removing one cause of the barons' irritation. Although Simon was a key figure in this reform movement he was not as yet its supreme leader. This is not surprising for, though an active participant in the parliaments of February and October 1259, he was absent in France for the remainder of the year, his attentions focussed on the Anglo-French treaty and on his own private affairs. In the short term, at least, this withdrawal from events in England threatened both his own position and the solidarity of the baronial forces.

With the removal of the Lusignans from the English scene some reformists seemed satisfied that they had achieved all that was necessary. Foremost amongst these was Richard de Clare, earl of Gloucester. As a person who commanded widespread support his change of heart was to influence others, thereby seriously dividing those who had made up the original baronial movement. Whilst Simon called these renegades "fickle and deceitful", his absence in France at this critical time could only have worked to their benefit. He too, for much of 1259, appeared to have lost interest in reform.

During this period in France Simon was absorbed with improving his financial position. He maintained, with some justification, that the king had failed to honour a promise to replace certain annual cash payments by an allocation of land. Returning to the dower settlement due to his wife as a result of her first husband's death, he argued that this had fallen well short of the amount due, with the result that a large sum of money was now owing to Eleanor. To Simon the resolution of such issues, like those raised by the barons, was a matter of justice. Nevertheless he was prepared to use the threat of Eleanor's refusal to renounce her claims to territories in France as a bargaining card for applying pressure on Henry. Although this tactic, coupled with his persistence certainly brought him some economic gains in 1259, the dower issue was to remain a running sore. In general, it is doubtful whether his national standing was as strong at the end of the year as it had been at its beginning.

A thirteenth century knight prepares himself for battle

Chapter Seven   PRELUDE TO WAR

For much of 1260 Simon's star was in decline. With the treaty negotiations completed he no longer had a significant diplomatic role to play. He won few friends by his attempt to use the document to improve his financial situation, nor for that matter did Eleanor. Their refusal to comply with its terms was no more than a delaying tactic for renunciation of their rights in France did eventually have to be made by both of them. Though events brought some financial gains they were still left dissatisfied with the latest dower offer. To make matters worse, during the year Henry began to reassert himself by mounting a challenge to those who had sought to reduce his powers.

One reason why Henry felt safe to do this was the fall in the number of those supporting the barons' cause following Gloucester's change in allegiance. An extended visit to France prompted the king to delay holding the Candlemas parliament, scheduled for 2nd February, an act that was in clear breach of the Provisions of Oxford. This move angered Simon, especially when his strong protest was forcefully rebuffed by the justiciar, acting on behalf of the Crown.

Simon did have one powerful ally at this time, Prince Edward. The heir to the throne was currently irritated by his father's persistent efforts to exercise control over him and no doubt enjoyed strengthening the bond with his uncle, another critic of the king. The friendship between prince and earl was also encouraged by the fact that Gloucester, currently no favourite of Simon's, had laid claim to Edward's castle at Bristol. Rumours were abroad, spread by Gloucester some thought, that Edward was plotting to dethrone his father. Even when, following Henry's return from France, a reconciliation took place between father and son, Simon and Edward remained on good terms. This was particularly evident from the way that, working together, they managed to engineer the replacement of key officials with nominees of their own. A major office to be affected was that of justiciar where Hugh Bigod, the current holder, gave way to Hugh Despenser.

Back from France, smarting from Simon's recent attacks on him, Henry decided, for the second time, to submit his brother-in-law to some form of trial. The charges levelled against him included both his attempts to delay the implementation of the peace terms and his hostile behaviour towards the Crown whilst Henry was overseas. An Episcopal committee of six, made up of two bishops chosen by the king, two by Simon and two "neutrals" - the Archbishop of Canterbury and the Bishop of London - would act as judges.

Simon, determined to defend himself to the utmost, was assisted by the scholarly Eudes Rigaud, Archbishop of Rouen, acting with the support of Louis IX.

In spite of an impressive build-up the trial petered out on 1 August 1260 when news came that the Welsh had captured the castle of Builth. Simon, ironically, was among those summoned to deal with the military emergency. As it happened, however, his services were not required, a truce with the Welsh being agreed before the month was out.

For the next few weeks Simon kept a low profile, reappearing dramatically at the Michaelmas parliament, where he was to occupy centre stage. By now reformist arguments were beginning to take a different direction. Instead of being primarily aimed at reducing the powers of the king, concerns were now focussed on easing some of the constraints that, along the way, had been placed upon the lords, to the benefit of their tenants. This attempt to modify the Provisions was strongly supported by Gloucester with whom, unexpectedly, Simon had just reached an accommodation. His willingness to heal the rift with Gloucester, coupled by a preparedness to back his moves to reduce the anti-baronial elements that were present in the Provisions, was no doubt the price he felt he must pay to gain Gloucester's help in stopping further proceedings with his trial.

The following year saw Henry even more determined to regain power. As a means of removing the recent curbs on his authority he sought papal absolution from the oath he had taken promising to abide by the Provisions. Anxious to weaken the Council, and possibly eventually to eradicate it completely, he restructured his court to ensure that it was one that firmly supported the monarchy.

His moves to re-establish control were helped by the absence for a time of two key players in the drama. The one, Prince Edward, had crossed the Channel to go jousting and to visit Gascony. In so doing he took with him a substantial fighting force that, to Henry's relief, removed a military body that could now less easily be used against him. The other absentee was Simon, once again in France, busy exploring avenues to advance Eleanor's inheritance claims. One of these led him to appeal to Louis for help, pressing him to act as an arbitrator in the case. The close relationship between Simon and the French king was possibly further strengthened by the fact that Louis's wife, Margaret, also had a long-standing dower claim against her father.

In February 1261, just prior to the Candlemas parliament, Henry took up residence in the Tower of London, anticipating the hostility that his aggressive policies were likely to arouse. At the parliament itself he charged the Council with usurping his power, though he was careful not to challenge the Provisions directly. Instead he argued that councillors had exceeded what the Provisions permitted them to do.

Henry's resurgence went from strength to strength. He showed his contempt for the reformers by inviting the banished Lusignan, William de Valence, back to England. In May he ensured his control of south-east England by moving troops into Hampshire, Kent and Sussex. He replaced Hugh Despenser, both as keeper of the Tower of London and as justiciar. To crown his successes Henry received word from Rome that Pope Alexander IV had granted him absolution from his oath to uphold the Provisions of Oxford.

Henry was particularly keen to undo that part of the Provisions that gave the shires greater influence. This had given the gentry a significant role in the election of their sheriffs. As he regained control of central government Henry was eager to replicate this success at local level. He dismissed 22 of the newly-appointed sheriffs and replaced them with county officers more sympathetic to the Crown.

Simon worked with skill and determination to counter Henry's moves, but with little matching resolve from fellow magnates. Although many were uneasy about the king's actions, few were prepared at this time to take up arms to stop him. Opposition to the king was seriously undermined when Gloucester, who had briefly rejoined Simon in protesting about what was occurring, once again switched his allegiance back to the Crown, won over, it was said, by favours from Queen Eleanor.

By 1262 it must have seemed to many that the Provisions of Oxford were a spent force and that the reins of power were firmly back in the hands of the king. Whilst Henry certainly had accomplished a great deal in outmanoeuvring those who had challenged his authority the future of the monarchy, however, was far from secure.

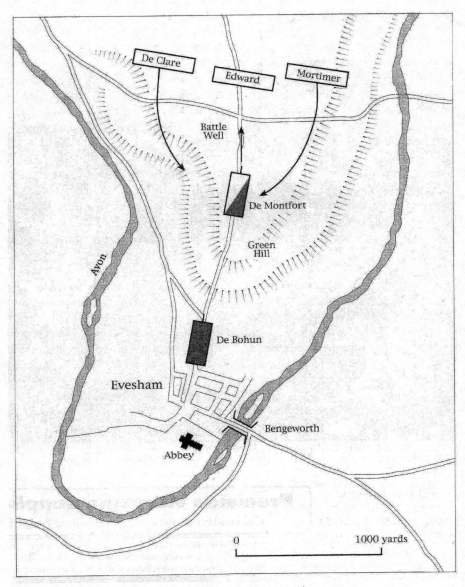

Sketch diagram of the Battle of Evesham, 4th August 1265

Chapter Eight   BLOODY CONFRONTATION

When 1263 arrived the reform movement had been under way a little over four years. Surveying its progress during that time it must be concluded that Henry, having lost considerable ground to the barons, now seemed to have recaptured much of the power that had been drained away by the Provisions of Oxford. The months that followed were to show that, despite his success in doing this, the royal crown still rested uneasily upon his head.

One thing that made the king ill at ease was the way that Simon kept him guessing about his intentions. Remaining in Europe, as Simon did, until the end of April, Henry was unsure what this absence boded. Did Simon seek the support of Louis IX in some plot to overthrow the English monarchy? Was he trying to persuade the new Pope, Urban IV, to rescind the bull absolving the king from his Oxford oath? Or had he, perhaps, simply lost interest in implementing the Provisions altogether?

Another problem for Henry arose from a revolt in Wales. To combat this the king relied heavily on a large mercenary army raised by Prince Edward. This need not have caused difficulties had not Henry angered his fellow countrymen by lavishly rewarding the foreigners who largely made up this force. English knights who had formerly served under the prince were among those who urged Simon to return home and do something to restrain the king.

Once back in England it soon became clear that Simon was still committed to reform. Indeed, he was now the undisputed leader of that movement. As such he was determined to make Henry follow the Provisions and organized the barons in petitioning him: "The Barons humbly and devoutly petition the lord King that the statutes and ordinances made at Oxford and confirmed by the oath of the lord King and of the magnates, and subsequently of all and singular of the whole realm of England, shall be firmly and inviolably observed".

Although a number of the magnates who had been key figures in the movement during its early days were no longer supporters, Simon felt confident that he had acquired new allies that he could call upon, if necessary, over the heads of the nobles. Amongst these were the mayor, burgesses and citizens of London whom Edward had alienated when some of his men raided the Templars' headquarters in the city and stolen gold and silver on the pretext that they were redeeming the jewels that the queen had pawned so that her son could pay his mercenaries. The Church was another ally promising Simon valuable support.

By 1264 what had to date largely been a battle of words was steadily moving to one involving military forces. At first this change was evident by no more than minor clashes between small bodies of men.

What seemed likely was that if these incidents were to escalate into a major confrontation, the numerical advantage would lie with Henry. The barons, ever motivated by self-interest, were liable to be split by personal feuds, often leading to unexpected transferences of allegiance. If Simon was to raise an army to do battle with Henry, he would not find it easy to gauge the size of the force he could rely upon assembling from this quarter, or for that matter, from such new allies as the citizenry of London. His confidence may also have been affected by the fact that his one-time friend and ally, Louis IX, had just declared his support for England's king.

The first major battle between the two armies took place in May 1264 at Lewes, in Sussex. Although outnumbered, especially in cavalry, the result was a resounding victory for Simon, both Henry and his son, Edward, being taken captive. The rebel army had strategically seized the high ground above the town of Lewes following an all-night march. Significantly, one wing of that army was made up of the citizens of London. Prior to the battle Simon had addressed his troops, telling them that they would be fighting for England, the honour of God, the Blessed Virgin Mary, the saints and the Holy Church. Present, to bless this "crusade", were the Bishops of Chichester and Winchester, underlining the help he was receiving from top clerics.

After Lewes desertions from the baronial ranks continued. His unexpected victory seems to have aroused fear, even hatred, amongst some of those who had earlier stood behind him. As never before, a number charged him with being an intrusive foreigner. As a result Simon began to cast his net for support still wider - to the town merchants, lesser landowners, the students of Oxford and to members of the lesser clergy disturbed by the growing influence of the Papacy. This was reflected, to some extent, in the parliament that he was to call in January 1265.

Doubting that the captive Henry could be relied upon to carry out reforms, Simon took the dramatic step of calling this parliament in the king's name. So that he did not have to rely entirely upon the barons for support, he summoned representatives from the counties and towns. Each shire was to have two knights elected by the freeholders of their county, while the larger cities and boroughs chose two citizens or burgesses. Simon restricted invitations to attend to fewer than half the leading barons, limiting the number to those who favoured his cause.

Simon's power was greatest during the first quarter of 1265. Thereafter, his support began to diminish significantly. A major cause of this development was the blatant attempts by some younger members of the Montfort family to use the current situation for personal gain. One of those who reacted angrily against this display of greed was Gloucester, who had become, for a brief time following Lewes, Simon's principal ally. Matters deteriorated still further for Simon when, at the end of May, Edward managed to escape his captors, though leaving his father still in their hands.

Hectic troop movements in the following weeks were to culminate in the cataclysmic battle at Evesham on 4th August. Although exactly what happened during this confrontation is uncertain new light has been thrown on the events of that day by the recent discovery of an account that was probably written by a monk of Evesham Abbey not long after the battle. As at Lewes, Simon's forces were again outnumbered. Unlike Lewes, however, it was the royal army, with Edward in command, that held the high ground on this occasion - one wing led by Roger Mortimer, the other by Gloucester - and was to emerge victorious.

The battle was one of the bloodiest fought on English soil during the medieval period. The bulk of the casualties were in the ranks of the rebels, Simon being the most celebrated of those slaughtered. Estimates indicate that at least 30 of the knights supporting the earl were slain. Among the dead were Simon's son, Henry, Hugh Despenser, Sir Thomas of Astley and Sir William de Mandeville. Not content with killing Simon, the victors dismembered his body and cut off his feet, hands and genitles. The defeated troops fled through the town and neighbouring fields, hotly pursued by Edward's men, to be killed when overtaken. In the report referred to above the chronicler describes how the Abbey church was "sprayed with the blood of the wounded and dead so that from the bodies ... a stream of blood ran right down into the crypts".

Simon de Montfort was killed in a savage melee, surrounded by his leading enemies

Chapter Nine   AFTERTHOUGHTS

The torso of Simon de Montfort, all that remained intact of his mutilated body, was buried by the monks of Evesham Abbey, close to its high altar. Almost immediately the former earl of Leicester became the focus of a cult. People began to refer to him as St. Simon. Within the first year of his death Evesham's monks recorded 135 accounts of cures that had occurred to sick visitors at either his shrine or the site of his slaughter on the battlefield. This response prompted Henry and a legate Cardinal representing the Pope to forbid any reference to Simon's sainthood. In consequence the monks were required to move his body to unconsecrated ground. Subsequently the number of chronicled cures diminished, with none recorded after 1280.

Simon, not surprisingly, has been viewed very differently by those who have assessed his life and achievements at various times in the past. Historians in the nineteenth century, living in a period of considerable political change in England, frequently acclaimed him as "the father of the House of Commons". Simon, both when helping to draw up and enforce the Provisions of Oxford or in his calling of a parliament in 1265, had no intention of promoting representative democracy. He simply filled his assembly with members he thought would follow his lead. He was keen to restrict royal power, but had no wish to give it "to the people". At the same time he believed that in government justice should prevail. It is certainly true that the concept of wider representation that he introduced did outlive him, to become a lasting feature of English parliaments. Those who gathered around the altar-like Cotswold stone memorial to Simon in Abbey Park, Evesham on 18th July 1965 - unveiled by the Speaker of the House of Commons and dedicated by the Archbishop of Canterbury - had little doubt that, if Simon was no democrat, they were certainly honouring a person who still held, 700 years after his death, a unique place in the history of British government. What he achieved helped to promote the idea that Parliament was sovereign.

Simon, as this brief account of his life makes evident, was a man of considerable talents. He was a skilled military tactician, a firm administrator, a widely travelled diplomat, a lively conversationalist, a scholar, an ardent Christian and a loyal husband and father. Quick-witted, there seems little doubt that he was generally more able than Henry. Many who consider his life will be puzzled by the way that relationships between Simon and his royal brother-in-law came to be soured to such an extent that they were prepared to go to war with each other.

The irritant that caused that relationship to fester was without doubt Henry's unwillingness - as Simon perceived it - to provide him, and his family, with a satisfactory financial settlement. The long-running disagreement with the king for failing to arrange a proper dower income for his wife, a dispute still unresolved at the time of his death, was one cause of friction. Another was Henry's failure to pay outstanding debts. Such an analysis, however, is in danger of over-stressing self-interest as the prime motivating force in Simon's life. Though this, coupled as it was with a deep concern for the welfare of his family, was very important to him, this complex person was driven by other powerful forces – a regard for justice, the need to lead a religious life and a genuine desire to promote both moral and political reforms. It is perhaps fitting that such a person should give his name to a university and that this institution should be in the city of Leicester.

○   ○   ○

I would like to acknowledge the help I have received in the production of this book from David Snowden, Iris Pinkstone and Stanley English.

The illustrations on pages 1, 6 and 32 were drawn by Iris Pinkstone.

The memorial to Simon de Montfort which was unveiled in Abbey Park Evesham by the Speaker of the House of Commons, 18ᵗʰ July 1965

FURTHER READING

Carpenter, David: "Simon de Montfort: the First Leader of a Political Movement in English History", History, 76 (1991)

... "The Struggle for Mastery: Britain 1066-1284" (Allen Lane 2003)

Gibbs, M. & Lang: "Bishops and Reform 1215-1271" (Oxford, 1934)

Hallam, Elizabeth (Gen. ed.): "Chronicles of the Age of Chivalry" (Salamander Books, 2002)

Harding, Alan: "England in the Thirteenth Century" (CUP 1993)

Labarge, M: "Simon de Montfort" (London, 1962)

Maddicott, J.R.: "Simon de Montfort" (CUP 1994)

Matthew, D.J.A.: "The English and the Community of Europe in the Thirteenth Century" (Reading, 1997)

Matthew Paris's "Chronica Majora" – a near contemporary account of events from 1235 to his death in 1259. Translation "Matthew Paris's English History" 3 vols. 1852-4

Vaughan, R.: "Matthew Paris" (Cambridge 1958)

Wade, M.M.: "The Personal Quarrels of Simon de Montfort and his Wife with Henry III of England" (Oxford B.Litt thesis, 1939)